EXPAND
The 7 Fundamental Steps To Grow Your Business

Wayne Fox

Copyright © 2014 by Wayne Fox. All rights reserved. No part of this book may be reproduced in any form without permission in writing from the author. Reviewers may quote brief passages in reviews.

Disclaimer and FTC Disclaimer

No part of this publication may be reproduced or transmitted in any form or by any means, mechanical or electronic, including photocopying or recording, or by any information storage and retrieval system, or transmitted by email without permission in writing from the publisher.

While all attempts have been made to verify the information provided in this publication, the author does not assume any responsibility for errors, omissions, or contrary interpretations of the subject matter herein.

This book is for entertainment purposes only. The views expressed are those of the author alone, and should not be taken as expert instruction or commands. The reader is responsible for his or her own actions.

Adherence to all applicable laws and regulations, including international federal, state, and local governing professional licensing, business practices, advertising, and all other aspects of doing business in the US, Canada, UK, or any other jurisdiction is the sole responsibility of the purchaser or reader.

The author does not assume any responsibility or liability whatsoever on the behalf of the purchaser or reader of this material.

Any perceived slight of any individual or organization is purely unintentional. I sometimes use affiliate links with the content of the book. This means by making a purchase, I will get a sales commission. This, however, does not mean my opinion is for sale. Any affiliate links listed in the book are the services and products for which I've used myself and found useful.

The reader or purchaser should do their own research before making a purchase online.

Contents

Introduction

What have you got already?

What's your Strategy?

What do we need?

Conclusion

About the Author

Introduction

Did you know that 90% of startup businesses fail within the first five years?

A fundamental reality in today's economy is that a business must grow or it will die. If your business is just treading water, you need to consider changing now! Inject some energy and life into it, or eventually you'll be closing the door to it for the very last time.

The title of this book states that I'll show you the 7 fundamental steps to grow your business. As I take you through the book, we'll go on a journey, looking at these 7 areas in much greater detail and discussing the options available to us one by one.

I wrote this book because there was a time earlier in my own career that I looked for answers that weren't available unless you chose to employ business consultants. These people were expensive, and for small businesses that's a costly expense you can do without. So without the money for consultants, how do you move your business forward?

I learned everything I know from trial and error: twenty years of my own direct experience and around fifty years of passed down knowledge from my parents' and grandparents' experience in the business world.

The things that worked, I used again, and the things that didn't, I either dropped or tweaked until they did work.

Within this book, you're getting a combined 160 years of business experience from people who have lived it at the sharp end, have grown multiple businesses from local small and medium sized players into major players operating nationally and even internationally, with most of them grown on a relatively small budget and covering multiple industries.

To have this experience passed on to you for very little cost is probably one of the best investments you'll ever make for you and your business.

What have you got already?

Before you can start any phase of growth in your business, it's first important to take a step back from the day-to-day business, and take stock of what you already have.

So many businesses try to grow when they aren't really ready. Perhaps the owner wins a "one-off" contract, manages to deliver it successfully, but then believes he/she can duplicate that success across multiple projects at once. Business growth has to be sustainable business growth. Note that when we talk about sustainable business growth, we aren't talking about being "green" or "eco-friendly," or about being kind to the environment. Sustainable business growth means growth that you can keep building on, growth that doesn't go away after you complete one particular sale or single project.

That's what business growth is. But your business can only grow when you know what you've already got and then perfect it.

If you take time to observe local businesses in your area you'll notice a small number of these businesses grow in size.

This is particularly true for service businesses as these are more noticeable because of their scale, with their vehicles and staff more visible to the general public. This phenomenon is probably more noticeable out of town. Perhaps you'll see a two to three person business grow to become an eight to nine person business relatively quickly. From this point, one of three things can happen, depending on how the business is being run and how it's been set up from growth.

- The business grows and then goes out of business from bankruptcy
- The business scales back in under two years to what it was previously
- The business continues to grow.

The most common event is bankruptcy. This is because the business doesn't have the resources in place to give it sustainable growth.

Depending on the business owners' own experience, often they win work pre-growth, and that work might only break even in terms of profit levels, but the owner doesn't know because they just assume their pricing levels are correct.

As the business grows, it needs additional levels of overhead to keep it running, supervisors need managing, managers need directing. If you have external investors, they want additional resources in place to oversee the owners/senior management, which all add to running costs of the business and reduce profits further.

If that growth is built on the same pricing level as pre-growth, without any additional investment for overhead and extra supervision, the owners will either be working twenty-four hours a day or the business will be losing money from day one of the growth period.

Often when a business secures external investment for growth, it will input the necessary team in place for it to achieve fast growth. This is okay because the business is set up in order to keep up with that growth, but it will need to reach those growth targets quickly. Otherwise it will lose money for every day that it doesn't achieve them. On one hand this is a fast way to grow the business if it's a proven model and customers are ready to buy. But it also carries a higher risk.

What if the business doesn't meet your growth expectations?

Will the investors give you more money?

How long can you afford to carry on without hitting your growth figures?

If your growth figures are based on incremental growth across a period of time, but you're down by say, 10% in period 1, continuing at the same level will see you down by 20% or more by period 2. If you've put in place the senior team to manage your period 2 growth expectations, but you're down by 20% on those targets, your running costs are 20% (or more) higher than you expected. How will you make up that shortfall?

Your answer might be that you won't recruit the period 2 staff levels if you haven't hit your targets. That's all well and good, but in reality you'll be recruiting these people well in advance of when you need them. It takes time to find the right people; the average middle manager takes between three to six months to recruit, and a senior manager can take up to one year.

The higher up the food chain you go, the harder it is to find suitable applicants, and these people all have to work a notice period with their existing employers. This means that to recruit staff for period 2, depending on how long each period is, you might be searching for and interviewing candidates from day one of your growth phase.

How will you cover the missed target costs? Will investors give you the funds to cover "bad costs," or will they just cut their losses and exit the business? One option could be to add the extra cost to your service/product line, but how would adding 20% to your existing prices help you achieve your targets? It's more likely it could drastically increase your shortfall for the current period.

An alternative to this fast growth method is to slow it down a bit and just take on the team as it grows. This can cause a sense of "fire-fighting;" as the business hits problems it almost seems like you're growing before you recruit the people to manage that growth. It's also a much slower way to grow the business.

As I mentioned earlier, you have to bear in mind the timescales involved in recruiting suitable candidates. If you don't recruit until you have a solid need for that individual, the chances are that by the time that candidate starts, you'll have a need for someone else as well. Every option can have its own set of headaches and frustrations.

My recommendation is that you use a combination of both options if you have the financial resources to do so. This might mean that you recruit for any role, particularly management, a couple of months before they are needed. This will mean a cost to the business, but you'll have that person ready to go instead of always chasing your tail. I've used this option in businesses myself previously.

Another reason for failure in growth is that when a business grows it recruits new people to meet that extra demand.

Often the resourcing of that growth is unplanned, and so recruitment is the very last thing to be done.

This means that the new staff get thrown into the work on their first day with very little training of how the business does things. The business most likely has little or no orientation procedures for new staff in place. So when things go wrong, the owners blame the new staff, and wonder why they can't find any good staff. By using a combination of training and mentoring, most staff should perform the work successfully.

One point to bear in mind for getting this right is to train your existing team to become ambassadors of the right way to do things. As the business grows, empower these existing staff to train the new staff in how to do things. You might find some naturally strong people in the business already.

Perhaps you'll identify these people as those with strong opinions of how things are done. If left alone, these people can damage the business. However, if you use them to your advantage and train them in how you want to perform the tasks, you may find you have a very strong leader, and someone who can effectively teach others how a process must be done.

Using this method of delegation reduces input from the owners, with just a process of auditing the staff every few months, or perhaps per contract. You'll know what frequency is best for your business, and it may be a case of trial and error depending on how much you find yourself stepping in to resolve problems.

All businesses need to grow. Think of it like a car. You drive your car, you have a GO pedal, and a STOP pedal. If you're not pressing the GO pedal, then you're slowing down.

Eventually you'll come to a standstill, and at this point the car dies. You can decide at what speed your car goes by varying the pressure you place on the GO pedal, but the most important thing is that you're pressing the GO pedal.

By pressing the GO pedal, the car needs fuel (that is, your resources, customers, and investment), but the faster it goes, the more ground it covers. It's the same in your business. Keep driving the business forward, or it'll come to a standstill.

To extend this metaphor further, imagine your business as a car race. The other cars on the track are your competitors. If you slow down, they'll overtake you, and take more market share from you. There is only a limited number of customers that you can have without growing.

If you could be in a number of races, you might be going slowly in all of them, but at least you'd be building momentum in each one. Keep driving your business forward, and take more ground than your competitors.

Growing a business can be growing sales/profits, or it could mean growing the sales channels, locations, staff numbers, or new products or services.

Growing doesn't have to be the hard and fast sales growth we generally consider to be business growth. It might simply be the process of evolution. When we talk about people growing as part of a learning process we aren't talking about physical growth, as in getting taller or fatter. We're talking about growing or evolving internally.

A lot of business consultants talk about a business needing systems in place in order for it to grow. This is an important part of growing a business, but it makes up only one piece of the growth process. Consider a business with every system imaginable, but zero sales channels. I've seen this happen to a few businesses.

Imagine a small high street shop. It's difficult for that business to grow in physical size without major investment (expanding into the next door shop unit, or adding multiple floors).

Such growth carries ultra-high risk factors as the business has to double its sales volume overnight just to pay for that extra space. Without considering the virtual online growth opportunities for a retail business, it's still possible for the business to grow without renting extra space, which we'll go into in the later chapters.

So what have you got already? Let's go through the essentials.

The Business Model

- What is your business model?
- How does the business reach its customer?
- How does the business make money?

Let's look at a typical business model for a bakery as an example. Perhaps the bakery generally bakes the product then delivers it to a number of resellers, or perhaps even small supermarkets. It might make money from every unit sold by the resellers, or it might act purely as a supplier to the reseller (like a wholesaler), and get paid on delivery.

Your business model encompasses the whole business process from start to finish. It doesn't have to be unique; there are multiple copycat businesses, particularly in the service industry, and that's fine. There is no point in reinventing the wheel if it works.

In brief, to know or perfect your business model, you need to know:

- Who are your customers?
- How do you create value for those customers?
- How do you reach those customers both in terms of delivery and sales?
- How do you manage the customer?
- How do you make money, and what are your revenue streams?
- What resources do you need?
- When do you need those resources?
- Where do you need those resources?
- What systems and processes do you need in place to perform that process efficiently?

- How do you resource your business?
- Do you outsource, partner, or just employ the staff directly?
- What are your direct and indirect costs?
- What is your break even point?
- What profit margins do you make, and how much on each product/service?
- How much can you afford to reduce your mark ups in the event of a price war starting with a competitor?

The Why

Why did you set your business up?

Why should a customer buy from you instead of a competitor?

This might have a deeper meaning than purely to serve a customer and get paid for doing so. Perhaps you have plans to change the industry for the better.

Consider your own passions. If you've read my first book in the series – *'SEED: The 7 fundamental steps to start your own business'*, you'll know I talk about starting a business based around your passions. I might add, those passions should be something that makes money, and you should position the business in such a way that you can enjoy your passion, but still make money.

The same advice is relevant here as well. If you're not passionate about your business or the reasons for doing it, you should change it, or change the reasons for doing it. You'll end up with a business that has a real mission, one that you can empower your staff to support and buy into daily.

You might follow the rules in this book and grow your business ten times its current size. But without having the passion or a "why," you'll probably feel empty.

I've been in this situation myself and know a few other entrepreneurs who have as well. I personally felt lost, and missing something in my life. Without passion, you never truly feel complete, and many business people often feel the same way, often going out to purchase material items in the hope of filling that 'emptiness' inside, but of course failing to ever find that missing piece.

As a last point to this section, you could also link your "why" back to your business USP (Unique Selling Point). This is the very thing that causes a customer to choose you over your rivals.

The Sales Channels

How do you currently reach your target customers to achieve sales?

What marketing techniques do you use?

For this section, I want you to go through your previous twelve months sales ledger. Try to understand where each customer came from, and how they came to know about your business. If your business is service based, this should be pretty easy to do. It might be a bit harder if your business is a high street retailer; you might have to do a bit of research, or begin now to monitor where customers come from for the next twelve months or so.

Your research might lead you to a surprising discovery. Perhaps your customers found you through a direct mail campaign, the local charity fund-raising event you sponsored, or maybe it was through your website via a pay-per-click advert on Google.

List them all. If possible at the side of each one, identify the cost of each one. For example, let's say you exhibited at a trade show. Your cost was $500 exhibit fee, $300 in staffing costs, and $200 in brochures. Your total cost to exhibit, therefore, was $1000, for which you gained 10 customers from the event, and perhaps 100 leads. You can break this down to costing $100 per customer, and $10 per lead.

At this stage make sure you include any direct labor costs as well as other expenses that you incurred at each point within your calculations. It might calculate that you directly mailed 2000 leads, with a very small material cost, but it took your staff 200 hours to do so. In contrast, a trade show had a large 'external' cost, but very low 'internal' costs.

By putting a value on the labor element it gives you a clearer picture of the best way to grow your business.

It's worth noting at this point that even if a lead has not produced a sale yet, it shouldn't be dismissed.

As part of monitoring your leads, you'll want to see the success rates per month, taking the lead from introduction through to a final sale, and you'll need to know what the average timescale is for each activity to convert the lead into a sale. If there are any follow up activities during the process, make sure you include the costs in your analysis, too.

Different activities can have different costs per lead. We'll discuss this later on in the book.

Next we need to look at all your existing sales channels. A sales channel is how you reach the customer.

If you place an advert in the yellow pages, that's your sales channel.

If someone regularly introduces new customers to your business, that's your sales channel. Perhaps you have a number of partners or introducers? Maybe someone unofficially refers to a lot of business your way. If possible, list all of these, along with measured results, costs incurred for each one, the number of leads, the number of secured customers etc. You basically need to gather as much data for analysis at this point as possible so that we have the information available later on.

The Team

If you read my first book in this series, you know how important it is to know your own strengths. It's equally important to know your team's strengths as well as their weaknesses.

As you grow your business, the emphasis will become less about you personally, and more about your team. You will not be able to grow your business if it relies on you being around, so you need to reduce your presence from it as soon as practical.

Aim to remove yourself in stages. Initially, remove yourself from the hands-on roles, for example, the day to day service or product delivery. In a construction company, this hands-on role would be the builder, carpenter, laborer etc. In a hotel business, it would be the chef, the housemaid, the receptionist, and the restaurant staff. Hands-on roles are the core roles, the ones that the business gets paid for performing.

To remove yourself, you need good staff who know what to do, and they know how you like it to be done.

A word of caution here, if you're reading my book as a senior management employee with the ambitions of proving your worth and growing your employer's business, removing yourself from the business could mean some disastrous consequences for you in the future for obvious reasons. Your employer's business may experience substantial growth. At that point you'll probably ask for a pay increase, or a bonus for all your hard work. Before you do so, consider this: your employer now has a perfectly running business, growth that is noticed by everyone around, but no longer with a need for your role, as you've essentially removed yourself from the business.

Will you receive a pay increase? Or will your salary be construed as an extra expense to the company now? My advice to you as an employee is to pass this book onto your employer, or start your own business. If you choose the former, positioning yourself as the future leader of the business is the best strategy. If you choose the latter, my first book in the series will help you to get started.

After removing yourself from the hands-on role, you'll remove yourself from the sales function if you're involved in that – assuming the service delivery and sales process are performed separately. To do this you'll need good sales channels in place. This may involve a good sales team. Or, for example, a hotel may involve booking agencies, and online booking systems which remove the need for taking hotel bookings on site. By utilizing the right technologies or partners, you can minimize your own time, freeing you up to concentrate on other areas of the business.

Finally, you'll remove yourself from the day to day running of the business, whether in task supervision or wider management. As the business grows, you can bring in more experienced people in supervisory/middle management/senior management roles. Realistically, these positions can probably do most of the roles better than you anyway.

Remember, your team is your business's strength, and there are specialists available for every type of role.

You may be the business founder, but that doesn't automatically make you better at performing a particular task than someone who's been doing it every day of their career for 40 years, and is potentially one of the best in your industry. If you know your strengths, you can build your team around you to complement your own strengths.

List each team member individually according to their name, location, qualifications, roles, experience, and what roles you see them best suited to. Next have them take the personality profiling test that I showed you in my first book. It's free, and it'll help them, as well as you understand their strengths and weaknesses.

To do this, go to www.geniusu.com. The test is free, and it will take only 2 minutes to complete.

At this point, if you haven't done so already, I'd recommend reading my first book in the series. It will help you understand your own personality, and give you the tools and your own personal strategy to develop your business, along with the key role that you should play in developing the business moving forward.

We'll talk about what the results mean for your team later on in the book, but for the time being, make a note of the results for each of your team members. You could encourage each of your employees to watch the accompanying videos as well.

If you work with a number of partners, and rely on them for certain areas of your business, have them take the test as well. It's important to understand the whole team, and how they might fit into it. Your business will only be as strong as the weakest member of your team.

If you spend time and money developing your internal team to a high standard, but your partner and external team don't do the same, it could be detrimental to your own business success. After all, if these external partners were actually part of your internal staff, you'd invest in them to bring them up to the same standard as everyone else.

The Systems

What systems do you have already?

Do you have written procedures in place?

How do staff know how to do a particular task, and get it right the first time, to the perfect expectations of you and your customer?

How do you review, test and audit any existing systems or procedures?

If you don't have anything in place to control your process, can you really blame your staff when they get it wrong?

The human element is the biggest cause for business failure. No two people think or interpret the same way. One person's "perfect" is another person's "mediocre." Explain things in intricate detail, write them down, record them on video, explain them again, practice them over and over again, test them, and then improve on any areas of weakness or misunderstanding. This is how a system works. You'll start small and expand outwards through the system until it covers every part of your business.

Many people associate systems with IT software or technology. That's a wrong association. Technology merely makes your system and procedures more efficient. It is quite possible to build your systems around existing technology and software, but even if you have software as part of your systems, the human element still has to use that technology effectively or it will be ineffective and an expensive waste of time and money. Ensure there are procedures for using technology, too.

The best way to know what you already have is to think about every task you perform, list them in numerical order, and then see if you have a written and tested procedure to cover each task or process.

Another option is to look for common areas of complaint or problem areas in the business. This will normally be areas where you spend most of your time fire-fighting or fixing problems. It can also be areas that staff and/or customers complain about.

As you move through the business fixing each of these, you'll find your life getting easier, with your staff and customers being increasingly happier with you.

By doing this, you will better understand what needs to be done to improve the business next, giving you a to-do task list which you can then allocate your time to. This is what's referred to as, working *on* the business, not working *in* the business.

Systems improvement is an ongoing process of testing, measuring, and improvement; don't worry if it's not going to be perfect at this stage.

What's your Strategy?

What's your strategy for growth?

In case you hadn't realized in reading the book so far, in order to achieve sustainable growth in your business, you need a number of pieces to your growth jigsaw, but you need them to happen all at the same time, while working in alignment with each other. Imagine the image of a circus clown, spinning plates in the air!

Okay here's the pieces to that growth jigsaw; you'll need:

Vision: Where do you want to go?

Strategy: How will you get it?

A Good Business Model: Is it scalable, and does it make money at scale?

A Reason: Why do you do it?

Multiple sales channels: Don't rely on one person to feed you.

Right Team, Right Seats: We're not playing musical chairs here

The Right Systems: Consistency every time

Strong Cash Flow: Cash is Oxygen to the business

Investment: Both financial, and your own heart and soul invested into the business. If you can have others in your team to also invest their heart and soul into the business, you'll be onto a winner.

Vision

Do you know how big you'd like to grow your business?

Is it an achievable and realistic goal?

Is it possible for a two person business to become a global business? Yes, it's achievable, but do you have all the pieces in your growth jigsaw to make that happen? Growing a two person business into a global business will mean making significant changes to both, your previous business model, and the way you think. Did the founders of Google set up with the intention of it only ever being themselves, or did they start out with the intention of the business employing thousands of staff across the world

This is your vision. Paint a picture of how you see the future when you've achieved your vision. What will the future really look like? What will it feel like? Imagine it in every detail. The easiest way to do this, is think about what you'd like your life to look like ten years from now, then think about what your business would look like to create that life for you. This stage is about getting in your time machine, and imagine living your life ten years from now.

If you want it to be a nationwide business, don't just say, "I want it to be nationwide." Be specific. It's not whether your vision is achievable or not. It's about being able to measure progress. If you can measure it, you're much more likely to achieve it. An example, you could say, 'I want to have twenty staff in every state." But you can get more specific by saying, "I want ten staff in New York City, five staff in Syracuse, and five staff in Buffalo," then follow this practice for each state.

The more specific you can be in your vision, the easier it will be to achieve your goals. It doesn't have to be just staff numbers. It can also be sales volume, presence, profit level, vehicle numbers, contracts, retail stores, customer numbers, leads, etc.

Another example could be the use of sales figures. Rather than saying, "I want 2,000 customers," describe how this is made up. For example, you might have 1,200 customers in New York City, 300 in Syracuse, and 500 in Buffalo, or it could be broken down further across each state. Taking it one step further, if you can access zip code data, you can break the numbers down by zip code. If you know that you want to secure 50 additional customers in Buffalo, break this city into zip codes. There are 20 zip codes in Buffalo, which means you only need a little over 2 customers in each zip code. Doesn't that target sound much easier to achieve? As long as you can measure it, you can probably achieve it.

The final step in the Vision process is to break down your long term ten year vision, and ask yourself what it might look like at different points on that timeline. I personally like to have a ten year vision, broken down into a three year vision, and then a one year vision. When you get into the next stage, it's best to then take one further step, and consider what it looks like at the end of the next quarter - That gives you a vision of what life looks like three months from now. Hopefully now you can see a clear path of how your life will build on each vision until you reach that end point.

The likelihood is that you'll miss hitting your vision in these timescales, it might take a bit longer, but by following this path, it will set that intention of what you want things to look like, and looking back ten years from now, you'll recognise a massive change in your life, from how things were 'back then'.

How will you achieve it?

This is the 'how' section. You know what you want to achieve. Now you need a road map, to get there.

The best way to start this process is to imagine that you've already achieved it, and break down your steps into very small tasks. Imagine yourself in the future looking back. What were the key things that made a massive impact on the path to you achieving your goal today. A good exercise to this, is to think about something you've achieved in your life already, then look back and think about the 3 or 4 things that you did, to achieve those things.

Example

Let's consider your goal ten years ago, might have been to start your own business. There were probably a handful of high level milestones you achieved along the way that directed you to where you are today. They could be:

1. You gained a qualification in the type of service the business provides
2. You gained a particular type of experience working for a former employer
3. You built a relationship with one key clients which enabled to you to start
4. You grew to having your first ten customers
5. You employed your first employee
6. You gained accreditation for your service, from the industry association
7. You secured your first major contract, needing 3 full time staff

With each of these seven headline milestones, you know that you had a lot of smaller tasks that you had to complete to reach each milestone.

From your work in the earlier chapters (collecting data about customers, recording timescales of the sales process etc), you have a clearer understanding of what you need to do. Replicate these previous actions, in a planned way to help you set small milestones. Breaking it into these small steps, you can see where milestones sit on a timeline, and which processes are reliant on other tasks.

If you've been involved in project management before, this process should be fairly easy as it follows the same principals. If you've got other staff, and it's possible to use their day-to-day work as part of achieving your milestones, you'll reach your vision much faster. Your team will also feel empowered to be part of the process as well as your business story. People like to feel a part of a journey, so use that to your advantage.

Let's look at an example for a service business:

Existing business: A small service business employing two staff members plus the owner, operating from three service vehicles.

Three Year Vision: To have 100 customers in each of three additional new cities. This can be broken down to opening a new city every year until you reach that three year target.

Milestones:

The first step is to break this down into cities. We want to focus on a single city first, assuming we don't have the resources to go into additional cities at the same time.

What should we do to focus on getting into that chosen city? Personally, I'd choose the nearest neighboring city as it'll be easier and cheaper to resource. You won't get lots of business overnight, so you'll need to resource it from existing staff.

Who is your customer? Identify all possible customers, identify niches if possible, and let them all know about your plans. Tell your existing customers about your plans, too. You may find that existing customers have a presence in neighboring areas or perhaps know people in their industry and may refer them to you. The next milestone should be securing your first contract in the new area.

Next you'll want to increase your sales channels in that area. Remember, you're resourcing the new location from your existing operations so you may have to invest in an extra staff member or two, or you'll risk losing your existing customers. Your strategy should include a plan to retain and grow your existing location, or else you'll end up just swapping your existing location for a new location.

The next milestone will be to secure your first 10 customers (or whichever measurement criteria you choose to use).

Keep growing new customer numbers like this. Your next milestone will be to secure your first 30 customers.

When you've achieved your milestone of conquering the first city, you'll know the process that you took, and you should be able to copy or tweak it for improvement as you develop your second new city. During this process, always be sure to retain existing customers and keep growing your existing operations, both in the original location, and in your first new city.

Remember: a business that isn't growing, is a business that's dying.

One way of managing your growth is to recruit suitable staff to focus on either the existing business, or the growth of the business. Either way the owner of the business should then concentrate on the other part of the business, whether that be growth, or existing business. Doing this frees up your mind to focus just on one area of the business, and as it grows, you'll find that if you stretch yourself in too many ways, eventually something will snap and you might just lose everything.

This is where knowing your personality type is useful. Looking back at the profiling system, if your personality strength is the Dynamo or Blaze profile, you should focus on the growth project. If you have the tempo or steel profile, you should focus on your existing business, and have someone else in your team (preferably someone who is either a dynamo or blaze profile) focus on the growth project.

After you've set milestones to reach your vision, you need to set achievable and realistic timescales for each city. I normally split the detailed section into months, and the wider section into quarters or years. Work with your team, using all personality types to come up with realistic timescales, using an 'Optimistic Success' 'Pessimistic Success', and 'Average Success' scenario tags as your framework.

In this example, you'll have each of your team members determine how long they think each target will take to reach, using each of the three tags listed above. Write them down in a table under each heading. Then average the timescales for each. For example, Optimistic Success might have 4 weeks, 5 weeks, 6 weeks, in which case you'll say your most optimistic timescale is around 5 weeks. Do the same for Pessimistic Success.

For average success, take the results from both Optimistic and Pessimistic estimates and take the average between the two. This is the timescale you should base your plan on.

The likelihood is that as your business grows, things will develop much faster than your initial expectations because some tasks should start to become more natural to you and your team. What I've seen happen in our own businesses is, things start out slow, and they tend to build momentum, a bit like a snowball effect, so to start with, it doesn't seem like you're making much progress, but over time, everything just seems to click and come together.

When we know the milestones & timescales, we can properly plan how we'll achieve each one. Again for this, just break down each milestone into small tasks, and if you have staff that you can dedicate to the task, then allocate responsibility for those tasks to those team members, and let them take ownership for the task.

In line with your milestones, set targets for sales and profit values at each milestone. Remember that if you can measure against your success criteria, you'll be able to achieve your targets much more quickly.

Strategy

There are a number of routes you can take to achieve your vision. These might include any of the following:

- Increase sales in your existing product offerings
- Add a new complimentary service line/product line
- Grow profit rather than sales
- Buy a Business
- Buy a Franchise
- Licensing

We'll talk about each one individually.

Increase sales in your existing product offerings
- Attract more local customers
- Sell to all previous leads
- Improve sales conversions
- Open a new location
- Increase sales channels

By using your previously measured data, you'll know who your customers are, and where they come from. If you know, for example, that since you get 40% of your enquiries from advertising in a particular magazine, you should increase advertising in this magazine or similar magazines.

However, when you measure further you discover that only 1% of these enquiries result in a sale. With this type of analysis, you can surmise that this advertising is either a waste of time and money, that this audience isn't right for your business, or that you're giving the wrong message in the advertising, leading to low sales conversion rates.

Add a new complimentary service/product line
- Identify what rivals are selling that you're not
- What skills do your team have?
- What similar product/service are your customers buying?
- Will they buy from you if you add the product/service to your existing offering?

This has been a strategy I've used in our own businesses a lot. My natural skillset is to create & package new product offerings. When we had our Electrical & Mechanical contracting business many years ago, it started out just providing basic Electrical contracting services. Over time, we created new specialist product offerings including a Fire & Security division, an Electrical appliances division, a Data & Telecoms division, an Audio Visual division, and a Smart Home automation division. These were all products & services our existing customers were already buying from other companies, so by providing them ourselves, it meant we became the 'one-stop shop', for everything they needed.

Grow profit rather than sales

- Reduce costs of overhead
- Reduce delivery costs
- Look for efficiency savings
- Increase sales conversions
- Targeted marketing based on only the best measured results
- Introducing or improving systems
- Outsourcing non-core activities
- Focus on the most profitable activities only (80% of profits typically come from only 20% of customers)
- Partner with other similar businesses
- Add 5%-10% to your sales prices.

There's a strong chance that some activities or product offerings will be losing your business money, or at least they'll not be as profitable as other areas of the business. The problem is, without knowing this you keep feeding every part of the business equally.

One product offering might need additional staff recruiting, so you feed in the investment to make that happen, but after analysing where the profit comes from, you discover, the areas you've invested heavily into, are barely breaking even.

By using your measured analysis from earlier, you'll see exactly where your existing profits come from, where you can tweak things, and what you can drop without damaging your business whilst improving profit margins. Raising profits isn't just about raising prices. If you can reduce your costs by 10%, and add 10% to your sales price, you'll actually see more than 20% additional profit while doing relatively little work.

Don't be afraid to add a little price increase to your sale prices. Will your customer even notice a 5%-10% price increase anyway? Let's look at my example below to demonstrate what I mean.

Pre-growth

    Sales $100,000

    Costs $80,000 (80%)

    Net Profit $20,000 (20%)

Post growth - 10% sales price increase, 10% cost reduction

    Sales $110,000

    Costs $72,000

    Net Profit $38,000 (34.5%)

In the example, we've jumped from a 20% net profit figure, to a 34.5% net profit figure. In real terms you've almost doubled your bottom line.

Buy a Business
- Buying a local competitor
- Buying a local complimentary business
- Buying a competitor in another area
- Buying a complimentary business in another area

Buying a business, if done correctly can be one of the easiest and fastest ways to grow your business. Consider if you purchased a competitor business, you'd effectively get many more customers, but you'd also get staff, and goodwill that's been built up over the years. You'll also reduce the number of rivals you're competing against. There are various routes to do this, and you may wish to keep both businesses operating under separate brands, perhaps having one pitched at the higher end of the market, while the other concentrates on the opposite end of the market.

With buying a business, there are risks to watch for, if this is your strategy, and any business acquisition strategy should be carefully considered to align with your business goals.

A similar option can be to merge with a business, where you feel a collaboration of interests may be present. Business acquisitions is something we work on a lot, and with the baby boomer generation making up 70% of all business owners, it means there's a lot of people hoping to retire between now and 2035.

Buy a franchise

Buying a franchise is buying the rights to use someone else's brand recognition, perhaps even some customers, additional service lines, market niches, system of delivering the product, etc. It means you'll effectively be running two businesses, with potentially twice the marketing cost. If there are ten players in your local market, and you own two of them, you theoretically have twice as much growth potential as any of your rivals. Another reason to buy a franchise is to reach a different type of customer.

For example, many national corporations choose not to purchase from smaller local suppliers, instead selecting a supplier with a nationwide presence. This is where a franchise business can be a shrewd strategy to choose.

Licensing

Licensing means that one company gives another company the exclusive rights to distribute their product or service within a stated geographic territory. This is very similar to franchising, except it is more commonly associated with physical products rather than services.

For example, if your business is an electronics retailer, there may be a new games console that has better features than other consoles. By becoming the licensee of this product, you get exclusive rights to sell the games console in your retail store. By doing so, you will have many more customers coming into your store to buy it.

This obviously has other clear benefits. Not only do customers buy the product from you, increasing your sales/profit figures, but they also may purchase other items from you during their visit. Bear in mind that you will normally be expected to market the product to the target audience within your area, so there is a cost factor in addition to the licensing costs.

Licensing can work in a number of ways. You might be expected to purchase a minimum number of units from the manufacturer during a specified period, you may be required to pay an upfront fee to the manufacturer, or you may have to pay an ongoing license fee such as a percentage of sales or cost per unit sold. I've seen many arrangements where a combination of all three have been used.

A much more common example of licensing that many people have probably experienced at some point, is when you purchase software for your computer.

The software company will typically build the software, and then sell it to you on a per user license. This isn't a reseller licence, but rather a user licence, but essentially it works the same way, as the licensor earns an income from every licence sold.

If your business creates products, licensing can be a route for growth. If customers want to buy your product, it certainly helps you with financing the growth, as most of the costs will be met by the licensee.

There is a more basic route of licensing, or becoming a licensee, which is through network or multi-level marketing (MLM).

This is basically where you become a local sales agent for a large brand. It doesn't cost as much as buying a franchise, and you're generally free to sell how and when you want. There are a number of companies that do this, but most of them are specific to the beauty, wellness or cleaning products industries. These include brands such as Avon, Kleeneze and Herbalife. Unless you wish to do this as a part time venture, separate from your primary business, I would only advise taking on such a brand that complements your existing business. If your business is a local gym, for example, you might take a wellness product which could complement your gym business, for example, maybe a food supplements or diet program.

To become an agent of a MLM company, you pay a basic upfront fee. This fee includes setting you up with sample products, business cards, a sales website, branded uniform, training etc., and then you're free to get sales. Various MLM companies may provide everything on a subscription based model, whereby you pay an ongoing fee every month. However, each MLM company is different.

What do we need?

We know exactly what we have already. From your vision and strategy, we know what you need in the future, (and hopefully at each milestone), so we're now comparing the two and determining what we need, and when we need it, in order to realize our vision and achieve our goals.

From the world of consulting or project management, this process is called performing a GAP analysis.

We'll need to look at the following areas of the business:

1. Grow your sales channels
2. Grow your team
3. Build your systems & processes
4. Secure financing

Your vision depends on how you'll develop each one of these areas, but your overall strategy should be to develop all of them together by aligning them under a shared target or milestone. For example, there would be little point in marketing a service to the manufacturing industry if you've trained your staff for the retail industry rather than delivering the service in the manufacturing industry.

Growing your business just takes focus and perseverance.

Grow your sales channels

Most people don't understand what sales channels are. They are basically any direct or indirect route to sell or to provide something to your customer.

This is where many businesses fall short. Owners sometimes believe there are only one or two ways to sell your product/service. If you aren't good at coming up with ideas for reaching your customer, employ someone that's naturally good at it. This is a skill that comes naturally to me, I have a spreadsheet on my computer which I update every Friday. At my last count it has over 4,000 ideas around growth strategies or ways to market a business.

We'll look at the most common ways to reach your customer, but this list is by no means exhaustive. In fact, it's only touching the edges.

- Direct mail
- Email marketing
- Website
- Ecommerce site (your own website)
- Ecommerce platform (amazon, ebay etc)
- Ecommerce price comparison site (Expedia, Booking.com)
- Podcast
- Online banner advertising
- Online PPC (pay per click) advertising
- Traditional advertising
- Partners
- Resellers
- Distributors
- Agents
- Franchisees
- Licensees
- Industry buying groups
- Referral networks

Grow your team

From your GAP analysis you should know what roles are needed, and which skill sets or qualifications each of these make up. After identifying these, you can see where you need to implement a training plan for those members of your team.

At this stage, I'd point out that if you want to grow your business, it's worth learning a little bit about employment law, as well as health, safety, and welfare regulations in your local area. Additionally, if you are planning to expand geographically you'll need to learn about these for each area you operate the business since the rules and regulations might be different.

It's worth working with a local HR (Human Resources) consultant, as they often provide various services to help small businesses in the recruiting process.

These consultants can also make sure you have all the right policies and procedures in place to limit any liability should a disgruntled employee raise a claim against you or the business.

Some consultants have various insurance policies available that will reduce your liability should a claimant be successful in making a claim against you. In most employment claims, courts will favor the employee rather than the employer, so it's worth bearing in mind that a little extra cost now may be necessary to avoid a much larger cost in the future. In today's 'ambulance chasing' society, there are many lawyers willing to pursue a claim against you regardless of the legal justification, so it's worth reducing any element of risk to you or the business.

Let's look at how each personality type plays a role in growing your business. As I've mentioned before, everyone can do each of the roles, so by stating them as a weakness doesn't mean that personality type can't do them, it's just not their strongest or natural role to suit their personality type.

To give an example of this, imagine two separate days in your working life. On one day, the day might seem to go really well, and time passes really quickly, you're happy and feel zero stress. On another day the time might pass really slowly, you might be looking at the clock every few minutes, wishing for the day to end. In this scenario, the former is because you're performing tasks that suit your personality naturally. In the latter example, it's very likely that you're performing tasks that although you might do them well, it isn't natural to you, and can often cause a feeling of stress or anxiety.

My own personal strength is the Dynamo profile. As you'll learn, the Dynamo profile is best at coming up with new ideas, but not very strong at getting into the detail, or doing things like project management, as whilst the job gets done, details tend to get missed, as the Dynamo profile is 'big picture', future focused. The first part of my career was spent in project management, and in highly technical roles, but my biggest passion, the times when I really felt alive, was when I was creating the new product offerings we talked about earlier.

Dynamo Profile.

Strengths:

- They are highly creative naturally coming up with new ideas, new products, inventions, designs, and reinventing ways to do things better
- They communicate with the "big picture" always in mind. You'll win them over by selling them the big picture rather than

- talking about the detail of the project or how you'll achieve it
- They are best in roles coming up with new ways to do things, perhaps starting a new service or product line.

Weaknesses:

- Managing a project
- Completing larger tasks
- Doesn't like perfectionism
- Impatience, they don't like delays
- Gloss over the detail of any project
- They hate small talk
- Low boredom threshold
- Dislike repetition

Strategy:

- Put them in roles where you need a fresh approach
- Keep them on new short tasks or projects
- Don't put them in charge of quality control

- If leading a project, ensure they have someone focused toward the detail of the task

Blaze Profile.

Strengths:

- Good at building relationships with people
- Promoting a brand
- Typically very extrovert

Weaknesses:

- Not good at the detail of a task
- They don't like paperwork
- They don't like to be stuck to their desk or in environments without people
- Can be seen by others to occasionally be over dramatic in situations
- They like to make simple tasks very complex, and generally magnify them

Strategy:

- Put them in a sales or people facing role where attention to detail isn't required
- Try to remove as much paperwork from them as possible
- If possible, employ an assistant to take care of their paperwork responsibilities for them. In choosing an assistant to support them, choose from either the Tempo or Steel profile types to complement the Blaze profile

Tempo Profile.

Strengths:

- Good at performing hands-on tasks
- Likes the detail
- Project Management
- Timing
- Getting on with the task

Weaknesses:

- They aren't good at creating new things
- They don't like change; they prefer certainty
- Their perfectionist attitude means some tasks never get finished.

Strategy:

- This profile is all about the WHEN: When will things happen? That is their strength; use that as your strategy for this profile. If you need a task which has a high level of detail, give them the responsibility for it
- In projects, make sure you have a Tempo profile to balance the detail and timing elements with a fresh ideas approach from the Dynamo profile. This will also help to move a task on, as Dynamos will always push the project forward toward the finishing line without caring so much for perfectionism. By balancing a highly perfectionist profile with a zero perfectionist profile, you can get a good balance.

Steel Profile.

Strengths:

- They love paperwork, numbers, analyzing data, measuring, and systems
- They like to finish tasks and perfect things
- They love the detail, and need to understand the HOW of a project
- They are typically good with financial management, systemizing, and organizing things
- Most people within this category come across as averse to people, are often introverted, and may be seen by others as "geeks" and "nerds;" they are often excited by the work that others often see as boring
- They are good at providing detailed analysis and reporting.

Weaknesses:

- They don't like change; they prefer certainty
- Often seen as irritated by the "big picture," profiles of Dynamo and Blaze, they need to

understand the details of everything before they buy into it
- Although they are good at completing tasks, they aren't as good at initiating a task
- They can often be socially aversive, and can be misconstrued by others as arrogance, though often their introverted nature just means they aren't good verbal communicators
- They can often get bogged down in details and need help to see the bigger picture.

Strategy:

- Good in back office type roles. They prefer quiet spaces, often working alone or in very small groups. Open plan office working is not right for them
- Put them into roles building or dealing with systems, auditing, financial management, estimating, managing cash flow, project management, IT based roles

- This profile compliments the Blaze profile perfectly, as they are opposite. However, due to being opposites, they may tend to irritate each other

Overall strategy.

It's best to have a team which consists of at least one team member from each group. As your business grows, it should be made up of mainly TEMPO profiles, who are the doers, or the people that get the work done. The other profile types support the Tempo profile team members.

Each profile needs the others around it to make a project or business successful.

To give you an example, DYNAMO's are the start of the cycle. They create and reinvent things. They need the systems or the finance available to let them do it which is provided by the STEEL profile.

They also need the sales and people relationships developed by the BLAZE profile.

The BLAZE profile is second in the cycle. People with this profile build relationships and teams, promote, and ultimately 'sell the ideas' of the DYNAMO profile. Without the ideas being created, the BLAZE profile would struggle to do anything. Likewise, the BLAZE profile needs the TEMPO doer profile to start the tasks, and to provide the timing element and detail of the tasks.

The TEMPO profile is third in the cycle. These people focus on timing and detail, on getting things done rather than thinking about them. They are uncomfortable selling things, and building relationships and teams; they need the BLAZE profile to help with this. If the product hasn't been sold, they have nothing to do. Likewise they need the systems of the STEEL profile to help them get paid for the product, and to keep things simple. The STEEL profile helps them complete the process.

The STEEL profile is fourth in the cycle. People with this profile like to make things simple. They focus on making complicated things as simple as possible. If the task hasn't been completed by the TEMPO profile, they can't set up any systems or make the process simple. Likewise, if the DYNAMO profile isn't creating or reinventing new ideas, and integrating the systems of the STEEL profile, there is actually no reason for the STEEL profile to exist.

No profile can exist successfully without at least two other profiles, but if they come together, they complement each other and become extremely successful in their mutual objective.

If you're starting a project, it's important to make sure you include at least three profile types within the project to ensure it has a good balance.

Build your systems & processes

Have you drawn an organizational chart for your existing business? If not, then do this now. If you don't know what an organizational chart is, think of it like a family tree or genealogy chart. After you've got a pre-growth chart, then draw another fresh chart for the business which is your vision. List every role that will take place in your business one year from now (or whatever period you're working on). It's a good idea to do this for your three year vision, and your one year vision. By doing this, you can see the roles that you'll need to fill, and when. This process is a part of developing your team. If you have set your milestones, you can do a separate chart for each milestone, so that you can have a better understanding of how the business will look at each stage in its development.

Next for each role, you need to write what each person does, and what their responsibilities are. Have you listed every task that happens in your business already?

If not, you'll have to work on that next. Spend a few weeks and go through the process.

Start by considering the lifecycle of a customer, covering what you do to identify a potential customer, marketing, sales, negotiation, securing a sale, signing the contracts, purchase order process, delivering the order, managing quality control, managing customer service, invoicing the contract, financial accounting, systems testing, and company compliance. With every procedure, there'll be at least one document, form, certificate, or worksheet to go with it.

For example, this might be a template of a sales proposal document, or a checklist for checking quality control. You might follow a member of staff around and observe them performing their duties through fresh eyes, almost as if it's your first day at work and don't know how things work at all. Unless you are a Steel profile, you might prefer to give this task to someone who is.

Alternatively, if you're a Blaze profile, you may enjoy putting it all on video, and being the face of the company. One strategy is to have the steel profile create the system, then have the blaze profile publicise it to the staff.

Think back to your first day, when you started in the world of work. Although the simplest tasks now, they might have been pretty challenging for you to do on your first day. You probably wanted to make your boss happy at the time, but didn't know how she liked doing things. This is your chance to step into those 'day one' shoes again.

Another opportunity could be to take on a new member of staff. As part of the training process with that member of staff you could shadow that process and record it.

Many businesses that document their systems do them purely on paper. Although I think it's important to have a written version of systems, a video version can also be useful. It's often easier for people to learn from video rather than reading it on paper. And in today's technological age, videos are available in our employee's pockets, through the use of their mobile phones and social sharing sites such as YouTube and Vimeo. Everyone has access to procedures regardless of their location.

You will still need the documented version of any forms or live documents but these are often available through the cloud & online drives or apps.

The basic idea for this system is that although the staff member should already know generally what to do, they can always go back to the document or video as reference to get the process absolutely perfect. Systems and procedures can be used to make the business more efficient.

As I said earlier, even with systems in place, you'll still get some staff who don't really want the job. Perhaps they're being pushed into it from external forces. You can't train these people to do things they don't want to do. They might do the jobs, but they'll have mediocre results, and if you employ multiple mediocre staff, the business ends up being mediocre, too. This can often have a demoralizing impact on other staff members as well.

This is something I've seen when we've employed apprentices in our business. For many, the individual was forced into taking an apprenticeship by their family, or because they couldn't get government unemployment benefits. Often families can see a particular job through their own eyes, rather than seeing it through the individuals eyes. *'Get yourself a trade, people will always need an Electrician or Plumber'* can be good advice, and perhaps it's advice the family member wishes they'd taken, but in an age where kids grow up with so much technology, maybe they see the future of the world very differently to the generation before them. Mix this 'forced employment' with having the wrong personality profile, and it's a recipe for a very unhappy individual.

By inputting systems and procedures as part of the employment agreement with staff, they agree to work by your rules. If you find they blatantly disregard your rules or do things their way, it can be used as suitable grounds for dismissal.

Think about the large fast food chains, like McDonalds or Dominos Pizza. They have a very specific process that's followed to create the end product. Go to London, New York City, Sydney, or Cape Town, and you'll get the same product, looking & tasting the exact same way. If your employee doesn't follow the process, that burger is going to look or taste very differently, so suddenly it starts to hurt your business reputation. Causing damage to a business reputation is grounds for employee dismissal.

Obviously it's always best to consult a local employment lawyer on this, and they'll help you do things in the correct way, but procedures and systems go a long way to helping your case while reducing any potential claim for wrongful dismissal by a disgruntled employee. If you also build in a procedure, by working with your HR advisor, it will prevent any junior or inexperienced staff member, giving inappropriate disciplinary actions to other staff, which would also leave the business wide open to litigation.

Secure financing

You'll need an element of finance to support your growth. By using your milestones as guidance, you can break down the costs from each section to identify what funds will be required to manage cash flow in the business. As you grow, you'll bring in new staff, and for a short period, this will stretch the business until it has a chance to recoup those additional upfront costs.

It may be possible to cash flow those expenses through the company's existing profits, assuming the business makes a large enough profit already. It will likely take a very long time to grow the business by relying solely on these funds.

It's important at this stage to do a cash flow projection, including your projections for any existing business, and adding in the growth portions of the business to that. By doing this, you will also see possibilities of juggling activities around to suit cash flow and to prevent the business from getting into financial trouble.

So what are the options for funding the business?

    a. Equity investment
    b. Debt
    c. Reserves
    d. Shareholder funds
    e. Pooled investment
    f. Grants

We will look at each of the options in order.

Equity Investment

Bringing in new shareholders can be a good idea for a growing business. Dependent on the investor, it can also open up new opportunities for the business in terms of opening doors to new customers too. However, the downside of this is that many investors will want an equity stake in your business, with some investors looking to take up to 80% of the total business in return for their capital. If the business is established and has good returns already, it's possible to negotiate a reduced equity level.

How to value your business for investment

The important thing to remember when valuing a business is to not be greedy. You aren't giving the business a *for sale* valuation; the investment value is typically lower than a *for sale* valuation.

Any investment will be made for the purpose of growing the business, which means everyone will benefit. Without that investment, the company will probably not grow, and in reality will not be as valuable as a secured investment.

98.7% of small businesses advertised on the sales market don't achieve a sale! The main reason for this fact is their size in relation to their valuation. This is because many small businesses are managed on a day-to-day basis by their owners, and for any owner purchaser this carries a great risk; many of the staff and customers stay with a business because of the owner. Often when a small business has been sold, or a senior figure in the business leaves, a number of other staff and/or customers will also leave within a few months.

If you plan to sell your business in the future, I'd advise that you significantly grow it first. In order to do that, you need an investment, and you need the knowledge and experience to achieve that growth. Ideally, you want the business to be making sales within the seven to eight figure scale in order to achieve a good sales price. There are other things to consider also, but for the moment your focus should be on growth rather than selling your business.

Let's value your business for investment.

- To put an investment valuation on the business, look at the average EBITDA (Earnings before Interest, Tax, Depreciation & Amortization) figure over the last three years
- Replace your own salary, with the equivalent market based salary for the role you undertake. Many business owners pay themselves a very low salary, so doing this gives a fairer picture of the business. This is called the Adjusted EBITDA
- Multiply this Average Adjusted EBITDA number by Two. This is called the multiple,

and for small businesses generally ranges from one to three
- This gives you a rough estimate of what your business is worth when it comes to securing investment. If your business has a large amount of debt, or is distressed, this will affect the value of the business too

Here's an example.

EBITDA:	$100,000
Your Salary:	-$10,000
Replacement Market Salary:	+$70,000
Adjusted EBITDA:	<u>$ 40,000</u>
Business Valuation:	$ 80,000
	($ 40,000 x 2)

At this point, I'd point out that in some industries there are different multiples used for the purpose of valuing a business. I've used three, as it's pretty average for most industries I've been involved in.

It really all comes down to how much an investor likes your business, and how quickly they need to see a return on their investment. If you're in the technology, manufacturing, or real estate sectors, this valuation can be wildly different. General small businesses can be valued at a multiple of two however, as most investors like to get their money back within a two to three year timeframe, with any additional time focused on providing a profit for them.

When considering this route, you should also consider registering the business investment under any government backed investment schemes. This will reduce any liability for the investors when they exit the business, and may attract additional types of investor to your business.

These types of schemes will reduce the capital gains payable when they exit the business in the future. They are good motivators for securing investors for your business.

A word of caution if you're looking for equity investment. I've seen many examples where a small business has taken an equity investment, and been left disappointed after three years. This investor will be your partner in the business. If it's just money you're looking for, I'd advise there are better options available to you.

When considering this route, you should consider what you really need. The investor should have experience in achieving what you want to achieve. I see so many people nowadays calling themselves an Angel investor, who have no business experience whatsoever.

They've simply cashed in their pension, or sold an investment property, and they now invest some of their money into small businesses.

Other times, even though they have no business experience, they'll try to get involved in how the business is run, telling the business owners what they should be focusing on.

If you believe that having a 'silent investor' is a good thing, think again. If you believe that having someone (with no experience) getting involved with the business is a good thing, you'll wind up feeling very frustrated, and from speaking to many people in this situation, wish you never even started the process.

My personal experience has been in achieving rapid growth within a very specific type and size of business.

I don't work with start-up's, and I rarely work with businesses over $30million dollar in sales. It's the sweet spot between the two levels: established small businesses, they employ at least three staff but they have proven customer demand & they're experts at delivery.

This is because I know who I can add the most value to in the shortest time, and that's what is important to me. I do get involved in the business, but only in the areas we are strong, such as building a solid foundation ready for growth, re-designing the business model, looking at new strategies to grow, finding ways to increase profits, developing new product offerings, building strategic partnerships, putting the right people in the right seats, building a management team, acquiring 'bolt-on' businesses, and generally working on high level strategic activities. Aside from acting as a mentor & coach to the management team, I do not get involved in the day-to-day running of the business.

Debt

Debt is an investment or commitment on your part to pay the money back to the lender. Unless you are certain of your planned projections, and you can almost guarantee having the money to repay the debt every month, it wouldn't be advisable to do this. Debt funding is only good as a tool to support cash flow, like a loan, an overdraft, or invoice financing.

In my opinion, it's not a good tool as a means of financing uncertain growth projects because you can't be sure of the outcome of the growth project. You've also got to make that repayment every month. You can, however, claim the interest portion of the debt as an expense to the business, and reduce the business tax liability. By taking on debt to the business, this will affect the value of the business, as well as potentially causing problems with your lenders if you exceed their lending ratios, which occasionally can mean loans are called-in at short notice - which basically means you have to repay the loan within a few days or risk losing your home.

The ability to secure a loan in this form will be reliant on the lender, along with the business balance sheet, and financial ratios as discussed above. The lender will often ask for the shareholders to match the loan funds with either capital investment or some kind of security holding, such as their house or other personal possessions.

If you choose the debt funding route, and your growth plans aren't certain, it could mean the end of the business, and financial disaster personally for you and any other shareholders if you can't meet the repayments. Unlike the equity investment route, most debt funders won't be interested in making introductions to potential customers, either.

Reserves

If you have reserves in the business, then perhaps now is the time to use them. I'd always encourage a business owner to use only part of their cash reserves though, as you still need a safety net should things go wrong.

Shareholder funds

If the business has a number of shareholders already, it might be worth considering that each invest the money themselves.

This would normally be done on a percentage of ownership basis. For example, if one shareholder owns 3% equity, he/she would make 3% of the required investment or else face dilution of their existing shareholding.

Pooled Investment

Another option is to set up an investment pool, whereby each staff member makes an equity investment. This could be on the same equity levels as stated in the equity investment section, but instead of offering it to a single investor, it's offered to either multiple individuals, or a legal entity set up for the purpose of joint ownership. If you were growing in phases, you could use this model of investment to grow the business on a per phase basis. This is normally called 'funding rounds', and is most often seen in start-up technology companies.

One area of concern for founders and early stage investors with this route is their shareholding gets diluted so much with every round of funding, after a few years of intensively growing the business, they no longer own any of the company.

This option is great to achieve buy-in to the business, it will be unlikely to help in terms of what other professional investors could do for the business, both in terms of experience and introductions.

There is an additional point to consider here. If a shareholder owns 15% equity or more, they automatically have a voting interest. Let's consider that the staff form a legal entity under joint ownership, and this legal entity owns 16% equity in the business. They would have a say in how the business was run. However, if each individual is given equity for a small investment it might be less than 1% equity per staff member. You get the money, and you also keep all control of the business.

In such instances, you do need to lay down clear rules regarding the investment (for example, what happens to a staff member's investment when they leave the company).

Also you don't want a staff member who owns 0.3% of the business suddenly thinking they can turn up late for work, or thinking they can offer the company's services to their friends at bargain basement rates, just because they *own* it. Sometimes a situation can do funny things to people.

Please note there are very strict rules around how you may or may not offer an investment opportunity, whether to employees or to the general public, and you should seek legal advice and support in your local area, before starting this process, or else you may face a prison sentence if you get it wrong.

Grants

There are numerous grants available. These are normally based on growth industries or around employing people.

These change all the time, but most of the time you need to spend the money before receiving it back as a grant. On many occasions, you must not have already signed up to the project, or spent the money before making the application either. This process can take a very long time, and it can require considerable resources to make the application.

Make sure the grant award is well worth the time it'll take to put together. I have previously spent around 300 hours writing a grant application, only to have it rejected on a minor point. It's worth bearing in mind that you might not get it after all.

Don't rest all of your business success on securing a grant.

The best thing to do is to search the internet for grants available in your area or within your industry.

Alternatively, you could ask your trade association or local chamber of commerce for help if you're a member. They may be able to point you in the right direction.

Whichever option you choose for financing your business, it should be taken with lots of prior planning. You may wish to run the different options through on a spreadsheet, as if they were happening in real time. View this in terms of sales figures, costs, but also what the balance sheet looks like. Imagine a scenario that you take a loan but then need additional funds later on.

What does your balance sheet look like at this future date, and will you be able to secure suitable funding based on your new position? When running the numbers, throw in a few worrying scenarios, let's imagine you have a few bad debtors. By running the numbers in this way, you'll hopefully be able to understand the scenarios that could happen, and plan your growth strategy around them.

Conclusion

Hopefully this book has given you some insight into some proven strategies to grow your business. The best strategy is to plan ahead before doing anything further. If you can focus on where you are now, then build a path and stick to it, you'll end up where you want to be eventually.

Of course you may hit obstacles along the way, as I'm sure you've faced already, but if things were easy then everyone would be doing them. You may have to change your approach, but as long as you keep your end goal in sight, always work toward that, the actual paths you take to get there aren't so important. Eventually you will get there.

Business growth doesn't just come down to money. If a business receives investment, it doesn't guarantee it will turn out great. Did you know that 99.7% of businesses backed by venture capital investors don't even make it past two years, so basing an assumption around growth on 'having the money' is just nonsense.

Having the right team, together with the right strategy is what ultimately makes the business a success.

About the Author

Wayne Fox is a business re-ignitor, industry disruptor, commercial property developer, futurist, best-selling Author, & investor. Director of the Enyaw group, a UK-based investment firm that invests in *'freedom lifestyle'* ventures. He is experienced in achieving 7 & 8-figure revenue growth across previous SME ventures.

My online links:

Wayne Fox Website: www.wayne-fox.co.uk

Enyaw Group: www.enyawgroup.com

Enyaw Capital: www.enyawcapital.com

Enyaw Property: www.enyawproperty.co.uk

Linkedin:https://www.linkedin.com/in/waynefoxuk

Twitter: https://twitter.com/WayneFoxUK1

Instagram:https://www.instagram.com/waynefoxuk

Youtube:https://www.youtube.com/@WayneFoxUK

Udemy:https://www.udemy.com/user/wayne-fox-6

www.ingramcontent.com/pod-product-compliance
Lightning Source LLC
Chambersburg PA
CBHW070300230526
45470CB00002B/656